A FRAGMENT OF THE PRISON EXPERIENCES

Emma Goldman

Publisher : BoD · Books on Demand, 31 avenue Saint-Rémy,
57600 Forbach, bod@bod.fr
Print : Libri Plureos GmbH, Friedensallee 273,
22763 Hamburg (Allemagne)
ISBN : 978-2-3225-7749-1
Dépôt légal : Avril 2025

Table of Contents

A FOREWORD

There was a time—and that not so very long ago—when popular ignorance and superstition looked upon an insane person as one possessed of the devil or of some other evil spirit. They sought to drive the "evil one" out by beating and torturing the insane, and often even by drowning, hanging, and burning.

We have fortunately passed that stage of stupid brutality. Today even the most ignorant man knows that insanity is a disease. But in regard to crime and criminals we are still in the stage of dark-age superstition. We look upon the criminal today as we did upon the insane fifty or seventy-five years ago. Most men still believe that by beating and punishing the criminal, by hanging and electrocution, we can drive the "evil spirit" out of him. This process is called reforming the criminal.

Yet common sense and all human experience prove that the criminal is no more responsible for crime than the crazy man for his insanity. The pseudo-scientific theories of the Lombrosos in regard to crime and criminals have been thoroughly exploded and proven utterly fallacious. Even if the Lombroso myth that the criminal is born were true, what good would it do to punish him? There might be some social justification for his isolation, but how could the criminal, if born such, be held accountable for his criminality?

But as a matter of fact—as modern criminology has proven beyond all dispute—the criminal is made, not born. He is the product of his environment, a child of poverty and desperation, of misery, greed, and ambition. He is at the same time the symbol and the proof of a diseased social condition, the miscarriage of perverted economic arrangements. Fully 97 per cent. of all crime is due directly to our economic institutions. The other 3 per cent. are traceable to the artificiality and neurosis of modern life, to the anti-social tendencies cultivated among the weeds in the neglected and mistreated garden of human life.

I have been in close contact with so-called criminals for a great many years. Yet nowhere have I found the alleged "criminal type," nor have I ever discovered the "real criminal." He does not exist. Crime is simply misdirected energy, effort applied wrongly. The average criminal is just the average man, generally speaking. If in any sense he may be considered a "variation," it is only because of his frequently superior initiative, daring and intelligence. His often anti-social activity is conditioned by his unconventional vocation, not by any inherent criminal or anti-social tendencies. I am not speaking of congenital criminal degenerates whose number is infinitesimal, and who belong in the care of the alienist. The vast majority of the so-called criminal class are thoroughly normal human beings, if the term may be applied to the type of man produced by modern civilization. I have had scores and hundreds of professional criminals, young and old, tell me again and again, "The only hope and ambition of my life is just to get a little pile, so that I can feel secure from want. Then I'd take my family somewhere in the country and live a quiet and honest life."

My present space is limited. I can merely shadow forth here a skeleton outline of this big and very vital subject. In a forthcoming book I shall analyze more thoroughly the sources and the psychology of crime, and write of the unique and interesting prison types and characters I have met.

For the present it is sufficient to emphasize that our whole social attitude toward the criminal is fundamentally wrong. It is the attitude of barbaric stupidity that seeks to hide its own shame and its mistakes behind prison bars. It has neither understanding of human motives nor sympathy with human weaknesses. This social attitude toward the criminal, representing the lowest human intelligence, is reflected in the management and discipline of the prisons. It is apparent that modern criminology has had a very negligible effect upon the popular mind within the last twenty-five years, for I have found the prisons of today in no essential way different from those of a quarter of a century back. Brutality is rampant; discipline is synonymous with the absolute suppression of individuality and the crushing of the prisoner's spirit and will. The atmosphere of our penal institutions of today is that of violence and force, of force and violence. With very rare exceptions, the spirit of humanity, of understanding, and justice, is a stranger in prison.

ANDER BERKMAN

THE STATE PRISON AT JEFFERSON CITY, MO.
EMMA GOLDMAN

Twenty-six years ago, in 1893, I paid the first toll for my opinions in the State of New York with a year's free residence in the Blackwell's Island Penitentiary. I found the cells small, dark, and filthy, the sanitary conditions appalling, and the general attitude toward the convict on the part of prison officials hard and cruel.

Terrible as these conditions were, they had some justification. In 1893 there was barely a spark anywhere to discredit the antiquated and inhuman theory of predestination—the Calvinistic idea that man is born a sinner and that he must expiate his sins through suffering and pain. This attitude toward the criminal and the methods of punishment rest on this biblical conception to this very day. Much more did that idea prevail twenty-six years ago.

Since then criminology has undergone a revolution. Libraries are filled with works on the origin and causes of crime, on the futility of punishment as a corrective of crime. More and more frequently modern writers have pointed out that crimes are related to social conditions, and that brutal treatment of prisoners makes them become more hardened and anti-social.

With a vast literature on scientific criminology and the widespread attempt to reform prisons, to humanize the treatment of the unfortunate social offender, one might have expected some changes in the penal institutions of this country. Yet in the year 1918 in the States of Missouri and Georgia, and for aught we know in every State in the land, prisons continue to be "built of bricks of shame" and

ɪilest deeds, like poison weeds,

n well in prison air.

ɪnly what is good in Man

wastes and withers there.

anguish keeps the heavy gate,

he Warder is Despair.

To be sure, the cells in the Missouri State Penitentiary, at least in the female wing, are larger and some of them lighter than the vermin-infested cells on Blackwell's Island twenty-six years ago. But even there the cells are never light enough except on very sunny days, while more than half the cells are in utter darkness and without ventilation. In fact, air is the most tabooed article in the Missouri prison. Except in extremely warm weather, the windows are rarely opened, healthy women are forced to breathe the putrid air of consumptives and syphilitics. During the influenza epidemic, when thirty-five prisoners lay stricken, we had to plead and fight for the opening of a window. To this day I can not understand how any one of us survived, except that the Lord "takes care of us poor sinners."

Yes, the cells are larger, the sanitation modern, but in every other respect, in the attitude of the officials toward the prisoner, the cold indifference to his needs, the methods of breaking his will, and, above all, the mode of employment have not improved, but are even worse than my experience on Blackwell's Island in 1893.

I cannot dwell here on the blood-freezing reception accorded each hopeless victim when the prison doors close upon her. That alone is enough to crush the bravest spirit and to turn one's very soul to gall and hate. I shall treat of this in my forthcoming book, dealing with my twenty months' experience in the Missouri State Prison.

It is the task system that prevails in this prison—as truly slavery as ever existed in this country before the Civil War—which chiefly needs to be exposed. The contract system of prison labor has been abolished "officially"—the State is now the employer. Yet no slave owner so drove, coerced and exploited his slaves as Missouri bleeds and exploits its helpless victims in the penitentiary at Jefferson City.

Two months are allowed to learn the trade, which consists of sewing jackets, overalls, auto coats and suspenders—tasks varying from 45 to 121 jackets a day, or from 9 to 18 dozen suspenders a day. Now, while the actual machine work on these different tasks is the same, the number of jackets in the 88 or 121 tasks is double to the 45, 55 and 66 tasks; hence double physical exertion is required. Yet the different tasks must be made in the same number of hours, without regard to age, physical endurance, periods of menstruation, when machine work is sheer torture to women. Even illness, unless it is of a very serious nature, is not considered sufficient cause to be relieved from the terrible task. So, unless one had previous experience in the needle trade, or a special aptitude for it, one's life is made a veritable hell, beginning a few days after commitment and lasting till the final day of release. No understanding for human variations, no consideration for mental or physical limitations, except for a few favorites of the prison officials, those who are usually the most worthless. The shop foreman in charge is a boy of twenty-one, who took up the art of slave-driving at the age of sixteen. He bullies and terrorizes the women, holding the threat of the blind cell and the bread-and-water diet over them.

The vilest language is used to the women, some of them old enough to be the boy's mother. Of course, he is paid to show results. The only way he can get results is through slave-driving methods, as well as by actually stealing part of the women's output, especially from the more ignorant, who are unable to do their own counting.

On more than one occasion I have seen this miserable foreman deliberately steal jackets and suspenders from colored girls who are serving twenty-five year sentences and from illiterate white girls. If they dare insist that they delivered their quota of work, they are punished for "impudence," in addition to being punished for "short" work. In view of the fact that four punishment marks a month reduce the prisoner one grade, and that a higher grade means speedier release from the prison hell, the enormity of this petty official's criminal thievery can be appreciated. Yet this man is considered fit to be in charge of sixty to seventy "criminals." It does not take much wisdom to find the greater criminal.

It may be argued that this ignorant and vulgar young man is only a tool, and therefore not to blame. Partly this is true. The State is the real offender, the officials of the Prison Board, as well as the petty subordinates who live by the sweat and blood of the social outcasts. The very first year the State of Missouri became the exploiter of the convicts' labor, the St. Louis *Post-Dispatch* reported that the salaries of the prison officials had been increased $20,000 per annum. No wonder the Acting Warden, Captain Gilvan—a bully and a brute who used to administer flogging when it was still "officially" in vogue in Missouri—once said to us in the shop, "I must have the task. You must make it. No such thing as can't. If you do not give me the task, I will punish you. And I punish cheerfully." Having the support and approval of such a man and the sanction of the head matron, a woman entirely bereft of feeling, it is natural for the foreman to squeeze and press and bully the task out of the women. But can anyone suppose that the foreman could lend himself to such brutal slave-driving, if he were not depraved himself?

It is utterly impossible to keep up the required speed day after day. The working hours are nine a day, but in order to complete the task, the women are driven to the old-time sweatshop methods of taking work evenings to their cells. In view of the fact that the cells are vermin infested, and the jackets and suspenders the prisoners make are sold broadcast and have already been handled by consumptive and venereally infected male prisoners, who prepare the work, the results can readily be imagined.

Personally I was well supplied by many friends with nourishing food. I am an adept at the needle trade, having worked at it for many years, when I first came to know the many economic opportunities in our so-called democracy. Yet I never could keep up the mind- and soul-destroying speed in the prison shop. Therefore I know what it means to the underfed women prisoners. Not one but emerges with impaired health.

If the contract system were really abolished, why would the State of Missouri drive its prison inmates? For a very simple reason: the State of Missouri, like the private contractor, does business with private concerns in every State of the Union. Proof of this is given by the labels sewn on every garment that leaves the prison. I was able to smuggle out a few, which are reproduced here.

Civilization claims to have advanced, and in no country do we hear so much about prison reform as in our own. Yet what can we say for the State of Missouri, when at the head of their female department is a woman in charge of ninety women prisoners who has control over their life and death?

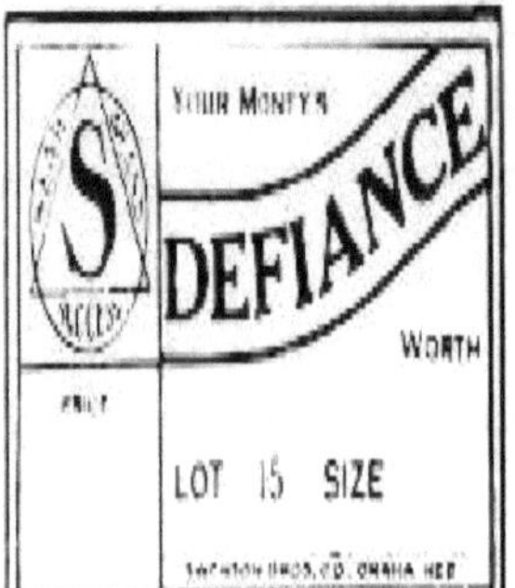
YOUR MONEY'S
DEFIANCE
WORTH
FULLY
LOT 15 SIZE
SAMPSON BROS. CO. OMAHA NEB

GREAT WESTERN
KUBITSHEK-SCHNEIDER CO
MINNEAPOLIS MINN

NEBRASKA SPECIAL
4000
SIZE 48

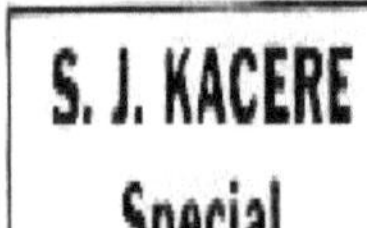
S. J. KACERE
Special
CEDAR RAPIDS, IA
Lot 838 Size

TRUE TO HIS COUNTRY
TRUE TO OUR TRADE
LINCOLN JOBBING HOUSE
LOT SIZE

The Iron Bound
FIT AND DURABILITY
C.S. Des Moines, Iowa
Lot Size 40

SAMPSON BRAND
GOOD WEAR GUARANTEED OR MONEY BACK
LOT 1025
THE CLOUD CO.
San Francisco, Cal.
Size 38 32

MAGNET
No.
BRAND
MADE BY
NORTON BROS. AND MORROW
LOS ANGELES, CALIF.
Every Pair Guaranteed Not To Rip
Lot 15C Size 38

EXTRA LARGE FULL CUT
GENUINE INDIGO DYE
194
KODAK SPECIAL
SIZE 42
SMITH, FOLLETT & CROWL
FARGO, N. DAKOTA
ANOTHER PAIR IF SEWING RIPS

This woman, Lilah Smith, has been employed in penal institutions since her fifteenth year, and has, therefore, little education or training. She is a believer in rigid discipline and punishment. She is really a neurotic, who has no control over her temper. She uses physical violence on the slightest pretext, especially when a particular prisoner is not in her good graces. Not once in twenty months did I hear her address one single encouraging or kind word to a prisoner. Flogging in the State of Missouri has been officially abolished, but Lilah Smith's vigorous slapping goes on.

There are three methods of punishment: First, the women are deprived of their recreation; second, they are locked up in their cells for forty-eight hours, from Saturday to Monday, on a diet of bread and water, and then expected to begin their task Monday in their weakened condition; third, they are sent to a blind cell, a cell 52 inches by 104 inches, with an aperture of 7 inches by 1½ inches, supplied with one blanket, two pieces of bread and two cups of water a day. In this tomb they are kept from three to twenty-two days.

Added to this maddening torture are the bull rings, which, while never used for white women during my stay, were used on colored girls.

The worst tragedy which occurred during my stay in the prison was the deliberate murder of Minnie Eddy. When I entered in February, Minnie had already been there a number of months. She struggled valiantly with the task, which she seemed unable to master. To avoid punishment, she used every cent her sister sent her to hire the task. In November, 1918, she began to complain of pain in her head and throat. She went to the doctor, but he ordered her back to the shop. She went back, but seemed unable to pull herself together to do any work. The matron decided she was shamming, and put her in punishment. At first she was kept in her own cell on bread and water; then the matron, realizing that we were feeding Minnie, transferred her to the so-called hospital, where a mattress was refused her, and only a bare cot and blanket were supplied. In that place the unfortunate woman was kept another week.

I went to the matron shortly after Minnie was put in the hospital, begging for her release. It was refused, the matron still insisting that the woman was shamming. Then, Thanksgiving Day, Minnie was brought down and allowed to eat her Thanksgiving dinner of putrid pork on an empty stomach. Two days later I took Minnie a couple of soft-boiled eggs, and seeing on her table a box sent by her relatives some weeks before, and which had just been given her, I warned her against using the decayed food in her present condition. But she was ravenous.

That evening some of the prison trusties came to me and told me that Minnie was in a heap on the floor, unconscious. I demanded that they call Miss Smith, the matron. The matron screamed at and slapped the unconscious woman. She was allowed to remain in her cell until Monday, when I could endure the situation no longer, and insisted on seeing Mr. Painter, President of the Prison Board, who came over at once. He had been told that Minnie was refusing food. He gave orders to have her moved back to her own cell, and put one of the girls in charge as her nurse. From the latter I learned that an attempt was made to feed Minnie forcibly, but it was too late. She never regained consciousness, dying Wednesday evening, at seven o'clock. Her terrible death benefited the other women, inasmuch as no one was afterwards placed in the death trap for more than five days. So do the dead sometimes aid the living.

There are two criterions on the part of the officials in dealing with the prisoners. If they are sick, they are told that they are shamming; if they cannot make the task, they are told they are lazy.

Frequently sick prisoners are ordered back to the shop by the physician when they are barely able to drag themselves along. This is the more remarkable because he is not an unkindly man and was especially decent to me. The reason for his indifference to the other women there I discovered during my last days at the prison. He is at daggers' points with the Board; therefore he is unable to do what he would like.

The Missouri State Penitentiary has the merit system, which is only another method of pressing out more labor from its victims.

Those who can stand the nerve-tearing speed and get into Class A, the highest class, have their time reduced almost in half. Therefore many of the women work beyond their limit of physical capacity to get out of the hell hole, even at the expense of their health. However, only State prisoners benefit by this merit system. Not so the Federal prisoners. They are forced to make the task every day, though their time is in no way affected. Imagine the outrage in the case of a prisoner serving a twenty-five-year sentence. Day after day, year in and year out, she is browbeaten and harassed to make the task. If she fails, she is repeatedly thrown into the "blind cell." If she succeeds, she gains nothing. The Federal Government pays the State for the upkeep of each Federal prisoner. In addition, the State makes a huge profit from the labor of these Federals. In return, it gives them not a single privilege. The reduction of six days' time a month is provided for by the Federal Government. It is a most unspeakable injustice toward helpless human beings.

In disclosing conditions prevalent in the Female Department of the Missouri State Penitentiary I am in no way prompted by personal grievances. Thanks to the liberality of Mr. William K. Painter, President of the Prison Board, and possibly also because of the fear of publicity on the part of the management, I have no personal complaints to make. In justice to Mr. Painter, I must say that he is a rather unusual man for his position. Whenever his attention was called to some grievance, he was always ready to remedy it. But prison abuses are conditioned in the very character of prison life and in corrupt politics, so that nothing short of the complete abolition of prisons will ever eradicate the terrible wrongs committed in penal institutions.

Meanwhile it is necessary to continue to point out that criminals are victims of our mad social arrangement, and to emphasize the utter failure of punishment as a corrective, as well as to expose the average brutal and ignorant type of prison official. The recognition of this may help to change our better-than-thou attitude toward the criminal.

As for my own experience, in all my twenty months of the closest contact with my fellow prisoners, I did not find one I could call depraved, cruel or hard. On the contrary, I know a "lifer" there who came to the penitentiary hardly more than a child. She has already served fifteen years. She is a most tender and devoted creature. She has one hold on life—a dog, whom she loves and tends with a mother's devotion. Who is the true criminal—this poor heart-broken little woman or the officials who have the power to let her spend her remaining years in freedom, and yet keep her? Another woman, who has a fifteen-year sentence, is completely broken in health, and in constant physical misery. She is passionately devoted to her only child, a little boy. Is she the criminal or those who keep her there? Her offense was the result of a moment's aberration; theirs is a cold-blooded, methodical and daily crime. Who is the greater criminal? Another woman, the mother of eight children, worked and starved half to death on a farm. She is thrown into prison for stealing a pig. Who is the greater criminal, this poor woman or the State which sent her there? I found no criminals among my fellow prisoners, only unfortunates—broken, helpless, hapless and hopeless human beings.

How rich in comparison are we political prisoners! Kate Richards O'Hare, who has the gift of going into the life of every prisoner, soothing and comforting and sustaining her, and is herself sustained by the ideal and the love of thousands. Rare little Ella Antolini, with her marvelous stoicism, her splendid fortitude, and her great capacity for human sympathy. We politicals are rich, indeed. Rich in the love of our dear comrades, rich in our faith of the future, strong in our position. But the others? It is for them we plead, against the wrongs, the inhumanities committed against those in the prison we left behind. Indeed, in every prison in the land.

A GOLDMAN

THE ATLANTA FEDERAL PENITENTIARY

STATEMENT BY ALEXANDER BERKMAN

Published in the Atlanta *Constitution*, October 1, 1919, on the day of his release from the Federal Penitentiary, Atlanta, Ga.

This country is at the present time going through the same throes of social and industrial rebirth that are convulsing England, France and other European countries. The steelworkers' strike is merely one of the symptoms of the social evolutionary process that may in the near future culminate in revolution. The sources of labor discontent in this country are identical with those in every other land of our so-called civilization. The working masses are not satisfied any more with empty political democracy; they demand a share in the products of their industry, and the opportunity to live, to enjoy life. Industrial slavery, perhaps more acute in the United States than anywhere else, is on its death-bed. The next step in the social life of the world is the taking over of all industry by the workers, both manual and mental, to be managed and operated by themselves, for the benefit of the producers instead of for the profit of our industrial and financial Kaisers.

The present struggle of the steel workers vividly calls back to my memory the great steel strike of Homestead, in 1892, when the Pinkertons hired by Carnegie and Frick shot the strikers down wholesale for demanding living conditions. In connection with the Homestead strike I served fourteen years in the Western Penitentiary of Pennsylvania. We have made some progress since then. The workers, especially, have learned a good deal since the days of the Homestead strike. They have learned the most important lesson of all, and that is that labor has an invincible weapon in solidarity. That is also the lesson that is being impressed on American labor today by the workers of England. Soon the

American Federation of Labor will realize that it is folly to call a strike of steel workers, without at the same time securing the solidaric support of all the other key industries—the railway men and the miners, for instance. As long as the workers in those industries strike separately, at different times, they run the risk of defeat. But a simultaneous strike of all the three key industries would quickly bring our Garys, Morgans and Fricks to their senses.

But whatever the immediate outcome of the steel strike, it is but a question of a short time before American labor will make solidaric cause throughout all industries and assert the right of the toilers to the ownership of the full product of their toil. The day of capitalistic autocracy is gone. The future belongs to the proletariat of hand and brain.

The present labor situation in the United States is full of promise for the future. The war and its results have proven a great education for the peoples of the world. They are sick of the high-sounding phrases about political democracy and self-determination that are in practice like so many scraps of paper. It is *industrial autocracy* that the workers of the world seek to destroy. This country, the alleged champion of democracy, is being daily changed more and more into the régime of Prussian militarism. The Government of the United States has taken advantage of the alleged necessities of the war to crush the spirit of liberty and to deprive the people of the last vestige of freedom. It has now become dangerous, in this free country of ours, to express an independent opinion upon any subject, except perhaps about the weather. Free speech and press are a thing of the past. The American junkers and plutocrats are swamping the country with propaganda for a strong militarism. Our industrial autocrats see the handwriting on the wall and hope to crush the gathering forces of labor by the bayonet and the machine gun. The voice of liberty is being stifled in the prisons. Our jails and penitentiaries are full of political and industrial prisoners who have dared to hold an opinion of their own and to express it. Men like Debs and others are immured behind iron bars because they love liberty more than they do patrioteering. It is to the eternal disgrace of this country that conscientious objectors, political and industrial prisoners have not yet been given an amnesty, though even some of the reactionary countries of Europe have long since restored their social protestants to liberty. If there is any manhood left in the people of America, they should immediately voice the most compelling demand for a general amnesty for all political and industrial prisoners.

Rebels against industrial autocracy, such as Debs, Kate Richards O'Hare, and others, should be the pride of the United States instead of being kept in dungeons. Woe to a country that has no Debs, Kate O'Hare or Emma Goldman! They are the voices that cry out the best aspirations of humanity, even in the face of the gravest danger to themselves.

Speaking of Debs, I was happy to have the opportunity this morning, before leaving the Federal Prison at Atlanta, to shake hands with the Grand Old Man of the New Day. If there ever was a martyr to liberty,

Debs is that man. How stupid it is of the Government to jail men of his type! Prison cannot crush their spirit, nor iron bars and brutality change their conscience. Their love of humanity transcends the fear of punishment or death. There are times when the scaffold is the most elevated position for an honest man. Ideals cannot be imprisoned, nor can the eternal spirit of liberty be exterminated by shutting up its champions in dungeons or deporting men and women out of the United States. I feel, I am convinced, that the future belongs to us —to us who strive to regenerate society, to abolish poverty, misery, war and crime, by doing away with the causes of these evils. And even in prison, where we cannot fight for liberty, we can always struggle for principle.

It is this attitude of the political prisoners in all prisons that makes their lot even harder than that of the average prisoner. It is time the United States Government should take its head out of the bushes and recognize the existence of political prisoners in this country. Even in Czarist Russia the political prisoner was recognized as a man suffering for his ideals. Benighted America still considers the political just the same as the so-called common criminal. In the Atlanta Federal Prison the politicals fare even worse than the average prisoner. A banker who got away with the savings of poor widows and orphans receives the highest consideration, while the man who loves humanity more than his own safety is subjected to special persecution and discrimination.

I find that very few essential changes have taken place in the administration of our prisons within the last 25 years. The same system of brutalizing and degrading the prisoners still prevails. Only the forms differ slightly. The dungeon (known as "the hole"), chaining up by the wrists, clubbing and shooting, are the dominant methods of reformation in Atlanta. Men are chained to the doors for eight and ten hours consecutively, without even the opportunity of answering the most pressing demands of nature. I have known men in the Federal Prison to be kept 21 to 30 days at a stretch in "the hole," which is a filthy, dark kennel, not fit for a respectable dog, and fed on two small slices of bread twice a day. Men are clubbed frequently, on the least provocation, and recently a young colored boy, "Kid" Smith, was shot dead for not walking fast enough while being taken to "the hole."

The average type of guard in the Federal Prison is far below that of the average prisoner, both mentally and morally. Excepting a few decent officers, of a humane spirit, the majority of the guards are vulgar, brutal and dissipated men. Some are degenerates of the worst type. At their head is Deputy Warden Girardeau, formerly in charge of a chain gang. He is a man of very low mentality who believes in the old-time methods of brutality and suppression. His tactics look towards the breaking of the prisoner's spirit and to the degradation of the inmates. A prison is the last place in the world, even at its best, to improve a man. But the Atlanta Prison tends chiefly to dehumanize the prisoners and to crush the last vestige of their manhood and self-respect. It is the Deputy Warden who is mainly responsible for the inhumanities and outrages practiced in the Federal Prison. He encourages the most brutal tendencies of the guards, and even frequently protests and nullifies the Warden's more humane attitude. The Deputy Warden is the most hated man in the prison. The inmates regard him as a religious hypocrite, insincere and mean-spirited. It is his custom, after reading Sunday service, to go down to the dungeon and chain men up to the doors. He tantalizes the hungry victims in "the hole" with the recital of the fine breakfast he had enjoyed that morning, and in various ways seeks to provoke them into some unguarded remark in order to increase their punishment. In protest against the murderous clubbing and shooting of defenseless prisoners, I circulated a petition in the tailor shop (where I was employed at the time), to call the attention of the Warden to the terrible situation. The Deputy, hearing about it, sent for me and asked me what my purpose was. I explained to him the general indignation regarding the abuse of the prisoners, whereupon he asked me my opinion of his methods. I told him frankly that his actions did not square with his religious professions. I said that he was cruel to the men, that he lacked all sense of justice and fair play, and that I thought—as well as the majority of the prisoners—that he was a hypocrite. For this I was put on bread and water in "the hole," a dark and filthy cell hardly big enough to stretch out in. After my time in "the hole" had expired, I was sentenced to solitary confinement for the rest of my time. I spent the last seven and a half months there.

The Federal Prison at Atlanta would profit a great deal both in discipline and morale by the immediate discharge of Deputy Warden Girardeau. Warden Fred G. Zerbst is a man far above the Deputy in every sense. He is a man of modern ideas and of much experience in handling prison inmates. He believes in the more humane methods of prison management as against the Deputy's system of brutal repression. Unfortunately, the Warden is almost entirely occupied with the outside affairs of the prison, so that the inside management is practically all in the hands of the Deputy. There is considerable friction between the two, with deplorable results to the prisoners. Very frequently the best intentions of the Warden are nullified by the manner of their application at the hands of the Deputy.

It is high time that the public get a look into the inside workings of our penal institutions. The amount of brutality practiced in them as a matter of daily routine is almost unbelievable. When will people realize that the criminal is a man more sinned against than sinning, a victim of our unjust social and economic arrangements? But after all, prisons and their methods are a reflex of the conditions in the world outside. With so much injustice, strife and brutality in the world at large, it is no wonder that prison life mirrors the same spirit. When we become civilized enough to abolish human slaughter in the larger prison called society, when we reorganize life on the basis of human brotherhood and co-operation, we will have no use for prisons.

NTA, GA.

ɔer 1, 1919.

ALEXANDER BERKMAN

REPLY OF FRED G. ZERBST
Warden of the U. S. Federal Penitentiary, Atlanta, Ga.

r *Constitution*:

In yesterday's issue of your paper you printed an article under the heading, "Berkman Charges Brutal Methods in Atlanta Pen," and which article is devoted principally to a personal attack on Deputy Warden Charles H. Girardeau. It is also charged that a majority of the guards are vulgar, brutal and dissipated men.

It is not my custom to reply to ridiculous statements or attacks upon this institution made by irresponsible individuals, but in this case the attack is somewhat along personal lines, and in justice to the men so attacked I trust that you will see fit to accord this communication the same privilege to space in your columns as that accorded to Mr. Berkman's foul and unwarranted personal attack.

Deputy Warden Charles H. Girardeau is a Christian gentleman of high character, clean habits and high ideals, who performs his duties conscientiously with a view no less for the welfare of those confined here than for the government under which we live. He has lived in Atlanta for a great many years and is known intimately by many of Atlanta's best citizens. I wonder if any of these people can picture Charlie Girardeau as a low-minded, brutal fiend who tortures his unfortunate victims in the manner described by Mr. Berkman. On the one hand we have here a man who has been in Atlanta business and public life for a great many years, always working to build up its citizenship and its institutions, always having in view the public welfare. On the other hand we have Mr. Berkman, who came to this country an anarchist disguised by the pretense of seeking the benefits of American freedom.... Mr. Berkman served a sentence of 22 years in the Pennsylvania State prison, after which he made the same kind of an attack on that institution as he has on this one.

Referring to the attack on the character of the guards on duty at this institution, the guard force here as a whole is constituted of good loyal Americans, who perform their duties with painstaking care, and it requires much tact and patience to handle men of all different mentalities and character assembled in a penal institution. The public little realizes the work performed by these men at a compensation hardly sufficient to live decently. These guards are appointed only after passing a standard examination prescribed by the United States civil service commission after careful investigation showing that they are loyal Americans, that they are men of good moral character and standing in the community in which they have lived and that they possess in a high degree the qualifications necessary for the position. If any great daily paper believes that these guards are of such character as Mr. Berkman describes, it would be well to endeavor to rectify the methods by which they are selected.

This institution is open to the public each day except Sundays, and many thousands of visitors take advantage of this and inspect every department. Unlike most similar institutions our isolation building, in which are confined men who can not be brought in any other way to respect the rights of others and the rules of the institution, is open to the public. Mr. Berkman claims that these "filthy dungeons" are cleaned up purely for the public visitors; if that be so they must be cleaned twice each day and it would not be possible for them to be very filthy at any time.

I do not ask to be exonerated on account of any improper conditions existing at this institution, if such do exist, and I cheerfully accept responsibility for its management as long as I am its Warden. This management, however, will be in the interest of the government constituted by the American people and not in the interest of a revolutionary propaganda seeking for the destruction of that government and the substitution therefor of the doctrines of Alexander Berkman and his associates, the abolition of all laws.

truly yours,

G. ZERBST, Warden.

REPLY TO WARDEN FRED G. ZERBST

r *Constitution*:

In your issue of October 4, 1919, Warden Fred G. Zerbst, of the Federal Prison at Atlanta, makes an alleged reply to my charges of brutality, corruption and incompetence on the part of the management of the Federal Penitentiary.

The outstanding feature of Warden Zerbst's statement is its entire failure to discredit my charges, much less to disprove them. I made definite accusations, gave facts, cited specific instances. The Warden's only reply is, in essence, "All's well, and there is nothing more to be said about it." That is the good old traditional policy of the authorities of all penal and other similar institutions since time immemorial. When facing charges of corruption and brutality, they resort to the grand gesture of waving the terrible indictment flippantly aside, with the too-easy declaration, "Nothing to it." But an outraged public sentiment, in numerous similar cases, has but too often exposed this high-and-mighty attitude as the invariable camouflage of rotten conditions within the prison walls. To cite but one recent instance, still comparatively vivid in the public memory, will be sufficient. I refer to the case of Mr. Moyer, former Warden of the Atlanta Federal Prison, who consistently scoffed at and ridiculed the charges of Julian Hawthorne (the son of his famous father) till the Hawthorne revelations of prison abuse and outrage, corroborated by numerous other prisoners and former inmates, were proven to the hilt, and Warden Moyer summarily dismissed by the Federal Government.

I appreciate the spirit of chivalry, of the *ésprit de corps*, that prompts Warden Zerbst to rush to the rescue of Deputy Warden Girardeau and his assistants, against whom my indictment is chiefly directed. I have emphasized in my previous statement that Warden Zerbst is more humane and intelligent than the Deputy Warden. I may now add that he is also generous, all too generous, to his official subordinates. But chivalry may be misplaced—it *is* misplaced in the present case. It will not do for Mr. Zerbst to barrage the outrages committed within the prison walls with his loyalty to his official family. He owes a duty, a prior duty, to the public, to the taxpayers that support the institution over which he presides. Besides, he also owes a duty to the men in his keeping, the inmates—about 1,500 helpless unfortunates—a duty he owes in the interests of justice and humanity.

To my specific charge that Deputy Warden Girardeau is brutal and of low moral and mental calibre, the Warden replies that Mr. Girardeau is a well-known citizen of Atlanta. 'Tis a rather lame and unconvincing refutation of my charge. To my indictment of the majority of the guards as vulgar, brutal and dissipated men, the Warden replies that they have satisfactorily filled out certain civil service blanks, or passed some other perfunctory examination. Yet in the very next breath he admits that "the work is performed by these men at a compensation hardly sufficient to live decently." In other words, the guards are paid $76.00 per month, and I leave it to the readers to judge what "high degree of qualification" $76.00-dollar-a-month men possess, in these days of high cost of living.

I emphatically challenge the Warden's statement that visitors are admitted to the punishment cells I described as filthy. There are in the Atlanta Federal Prison *two kinds* of punishment cells, known respectively as the "dark hole" and the "light hole." The difference between the two is extreme. The "light hole" is a comparatively large cell with a window admitting some light and air. The "dark hole" is a veritable kennel, wedge-shaped, about 2½ feet wide at the entrance, 4½ feet at the back, and 6 feet long. The prisoner is forced to sleep in this dark hole on the floor, on a filthy mattress, with a bit of rag for covering even in the coldest winter. Its only toilet facilities is an iron pail, sharp-edged, without any lid, the pail remaining in the cell 24 hours daily. It is emptied but once a day in the early morning. That's the filthy dungeon referred to in my first statement in the "Constitution," and I challenge the authorities of the prison to deny its existence, to deny that men are kept there for thirty days consecutively and sometimes longer, on an insufficient bread and water diet. No visitors, except government officials, or personal friends of the prison authorities, are ever permitted even a glance into this dark dungeon.

Can Warden Zerbst successfully deny the above facts? Even a most superficial investigation would bear me out. Can the Warden contradict my charges that prisoners are strung up by the wrists for 8 to 12 hours at a stretch, for 5 to 10 consecutive days? In his statement in the "Constitution" the Warden fails to deny that men are frequently clubbed, nor does he even refer to the unprovoked murder of "Kid" Smith by Officer Dean on February 21, 1919. What is the Warden's reply to these direct charges? His reply is that "Berkman came to this country as an Anarchist, disguised by the pretence of seeking the benefits of American freedom." A rather peculiar justification for prison brutalities! As a matter of fact, I came to this country about 32 years ago, a mere boy of 17, at which time I had never heard the word Anarchist, nor knew its meaning. I became an

Anarchist in this country, and it was just such methods as used by Deputy Warden Girardeau—the methods of tyranny, oppression and persecution, practiced not only in penitentiaries, but also in the larger prison called the world—that made me an Anarchist who seeks more humane forms of social life.

Warden Zerbst pretends to believe my charges against the institution to be but a "ridiculous attack somewhat along personal lines." Why ridiculous? Have such things never happened before in prison? Have penal institutions never been known to resort to brutal methods, or are prison guards generally acknowledged to be the cream of human kindness, understanding, and good judgment? Or are "the high moral and intellectual qualifications" of 76-dollar-a-month men beyond question or dispute?

The Warden states that I had made similar charges after my release from the Western Penitentiary of Pennsylvania. But he forgets to add that as a result of my indictment of the brutalities practiced in that prison, investigations took place, my charges sustained, and practically the whole administration of the Western Penitentiary radically changed.

As a matter of fact, I did not yet tell one-hundredth part of the terrible things that happen in the daily routine of the Atlanta Federal Prison. For lack of time and space I did not even mention the criminal neglect of sick prisoners, the deliberate starvation of the consumptive Nicholas Zogg, who is actually dying on his feet for lack of proper diet (he being a vegetarian), the unwholesome food, the vile manner in which it is served to the inmates, the favoritism of men with a "pull," the discrimination against political offenders, the corrupt system of "stool pigeons," the fake trials at which the word of one drunken guard outweighs that of a dozen soldiers, political prisoners and other inmates of character and integrity, whose sole crime consisted in the expression of an unpopular opinion during the war. I have not yet referred to the traffic, by guards and other officials, in cocaine, morphine, and other "dope," nor to the new 400-loom duck mill, the product of which is about to come in competition with free labor. Nor have I yet even hinted at the existence and the actual encouragement of homosexual practices and other sex aberrations resulting from suppression. I have not started yet, Mr. Zerbst, but I *will*, and that very soon.

Are these charges just "a personal attack?" Why try to mislead the public? Most intelligent men *know* that there are terrible abuses practiced in penal institutions. There are several investigations of penitentiaries and insane asylums going on at this very moment. The Federal Prison at Atlanta is no exception, and my attack is not directed against any particular individual, but against the system of tyranny, injustice and brutality inside our prisons, as well as outside. I want to do whatever lies in my power to ameliorate the conditions under which my unfortunate fellow-men in prisons have to suffer. I think that Warden Zerbst, as a matter of common humanity, should be the first to aid my efforts. As the initial step toward this he should eliminate all physical violence, abolish chaining up and the stool-pigeon system, and try to secure a living wage for the prison guards. You can't live these days on $76.00 a month. Most of the guards are married men, with families. Within the last two years a large number of new keepers have been engaged by the penitentiary, displacing the old and outworn men—engaged at $76.00 a month, with disastrous results to the inmates. The struggle for existence makes the guards surly, cranky, and quarrelsome, constantly conscious of their grievance because of their low pay, with the tendency to vent their misery and ill-humor upon the unfortunates in their power. The human element is of vital importance in prison life.

As a matter of common decency and fellow-feeling, in the interest of both the prisoners and society, I shall be happy to contribute my little share to bring a bit of sunshine into the dark night of the boys I left behind.

YORK,

ber 5, 1919.

ANDER BERKMAN

PERSECUTION OF POLITICALS

Practically every political and industrial prisoner in the Federal Penitentiary at Atlanta, with the exception of Eugene V. Debs, has been the victim of special discrimination and persecution. In the case of Debs, the authorities considered it best, owing to his great popularity, to assign him to the hospital, where he enjoys better food and treatment, without any particular work to do. At the same time this partial isolation of Eugene V. Debs from the rest of the prisoners precludes opportunity on his part for spreading his ideas among the inmates.

With the sole exception of Eugene V. Debs, all the other political prisoners in the Atlanta penitentiary have suffered special persecution:

A. Hennecy, a young Socialist from Ohio, was kept in complete solitude and isolation for eight consecutive months. He was allowed neither to receive or send mail, no books or papers of any kind, nor was he permitted work or exercise, or any other privileges usually accorded the average prisoner. The "crime" for which he was being thus inhumanly punished was, according to the official report of officer Demoss (formerly whipping master in the Atlanta prison), "Conversing in a suspicious manner with another prisoner in the yard, the other prisoner being Louis Kramer." Both Hennecy and Kramer were at that time employed in the prison shops and permitted, like the other inmates, to be out in the yard every Saturday and Sunday afternoon, privileged to speak to anyone.

A. Hennecy is now finishing a one-year sentence in the Delaware County Jail, Ohio, having been released from the Atlanta prison in February, 1919. He served in Atlanta two years on the charge of obstructing the draft. His present sentence is the result of his failure to register on June 4th, 1917.

Walter Hershberger, a conscientious objector, serving 20 years for refusing to don a military uniform. (His sentence has since been reduced to four years.) Herschberger has been kept in solitary confinement and isolation almost continuously since the early part of December, 1918. His solitary is "broken" by frequent visits to the dungeon, a dark hole 2½×4½×6 feet, where he is kept on an insufficient bread-and-water diet for periods ranging from 3 to 15 days. He was in isolation when I left the prison on October 1st, 1919.

Nicholas Zenn Zogg (spelled on the prison records Zough) serving ten years on the charge of aiding a young man to evade the draft. He was transferred to the Atlanta penitentiary from the Federal prison at McNeill's Island, State of Washington. Zogg is in the last stages of tuberculosis, and is being practically starved to death by the refusal of the authorities to permit him to buy or to receive suitable food from friends. He has been a strict vegetarian all his life, as were his father and grandfather before him, and he is neither physically nor conscientiously able to partake of the regular prison diet. He is forced to live mostly on oatmeal, badly prepared and served in the most unpalatable manner. Notwithstanding the fact that Zogg is barely able to walk about, he has been repeatedly thrown into the dungeon for alleged breaches of discipline.

Jack Randolph, an I. W. W., serving 10 years for opposition to the war, is in very delicate health and unable to perform the amount of work demanded of him in the tailor shop, was repeatedly punished in the dungeon and in solitary.

"Red" Massey, an I. W. W., from New Orleans, sent to the Atlanta prison on a frame-up charge under the Mann Act. This man has been kept in solitary and in isolation almost continuously for a year, and punished in the dungeon on the slightest pretext.

Morris Becker, sentenced to 20 months on the charge of conspiracy against the draft. This young man, of very slight physique, weighing about 100 pounds, and for over a year unable to eat anything except bread and oatmeal because of his poor physical condition and also because he was a vegetarian, was ordered to do yard work.

His job consisted in wheeling a large wheelbarrow full of bricks and cement up a very steep incline. Becker was unable to perform the work. For his "refusal to work" he was sent to the dungeon and there kept for 21 days on two slices of bread and water a day. He was released from the dungeon almost half dead, whereupon the authorities admitted that he was unable to perform the hard toil allotted to him. He was then assigned to the tailor shop.

Louis Kramer, serving 2 years for conspiracy to obstruct the draft, assigned, like Becker, to the same yard work, and equally unable to perform the task. Kept in the dungeon 21 days on bread and water. Subsequently repeatedly punished in the dark cell on the slightest or no provocation, chained up by the wrists to the door, and kept in isolation for 5 months till his discharge in June, 1919.

Louis Kramer is now serving one year in the Essex County Penitentiary, N. J., for refusing to register.

Alexander Berkman, sentenced to 2 years on the charge of conspiracy to obstruct the draft. Kept in the dungeon for five days on bread and water for circulating a petition in the tailor shop, protesting to the Warden against the brutal clubbings of defenceless prisoners; also in protest against the unprovoked murder of "Kid" Smith by Officer Dean. Sentenced to solitary and isolation for 7½ months, for calling the attention of Deputy Warden Girardeau to the brutalities practiced by the keepers in his charge, and for calling the Deputy a hypocrite. Kept thirty consecutive hours in the "dark hole" with the blind door on, which almost absolutely excludes all light and air, with the result that the man thus punished is put through the torture of gradual suffocation,—one of the worst forms of punishment known in prison life. During three months forbidden to receive or send mail, read papers or books, or to have any exercise whatever. Held in solitary and in isolation continuously from February 21st, to the day of discharge, October 1st, 1919.

As an instance of wilful brutality practiced upon the ordinary prisoner, I may cite the case of A. Popoff. In the latter part of 1917, while in a state of temporary mental aberration, Popoff killed a former Deputy Warden of the prison. He was taken out for trial and sentenced to life imprisonment. Upon his return from the court, the Atlanta penitentiary authorities confined him in a dark dungeon and kept him there continuously for two years, most of the time on a bread-and-water diet. Almost every week Popoff was subjected to a terrific beating by several guards, after which he would be carried to the hospital unconscious, and later again returned to the dungeon. This treatment was kept up from 1917 till August, 1919. Popoff became a raving maniac, and still his punishment in the dungeon continued. Finally, in the latter part of 1919, he was transferred to an insane asylum.

This is one of the instances of a prisoner of infantile mentality being deliberately driven into insanity by torture and by barbaric treatment.

This is but a small fragment of the numerous brutalities practiced daily in the U. S. Penitentiary at Atlanta, Ga. The lot of the average prisoner is hard enough, but the politicals are particularly discriminated against in the matter of work, of general treatment, and specifically in relation to their mail privileges. A young keeper, whose education does not exceed the three R's, is the chief prison censor, with the result that most of the mail sent to the politicals never reaches its destination.

In the daily routine of prison life, there are many and various opportunities to make the existence of the inmates unbearable. In Atlanta there are quite a number of petty officials, from the Deputy down, who make the best of these opportunities, especially in regard to the politicals. To the average prison keeper, the political offender is a non-understandable thing. He knows that the convict is either a murderer, robber or a thief, but that a man should be willing to go to prison for no material benefit to himself, is beyond his ken. That one should risk his liberty merely for the sake of ideas or ideals, is almost beyond belief and is positive proof —in the eyes of the average prison keeper —that the man is either crazy or hopelessly depraved. Such a man need expect neither understanding, sympathy, nor mercy. The average man is inclined to distrust and hate the thing he does not understand, and we always try to suppress the thing we hate. Hence, the more than usually inhumane and brutal treatment of the political prisoners in the penal institutions of America.

ANDER BERKMAN

IN CONCLUSION

The results attained by penal institutions are the very opposite of the ends sought. The modern form of "civilized" revenge kills, figuratively speaking, the enemy of the individual citizen, but it breeds in his place the enemy of society. The prisoner of the State does not regard the person he injured as his particular enemy—as did the member of the primitive tribe, for instance, feeling the wrath and revenge of the wronged one. Instead, he looks upon the State as his direct punisher; in the representatives of the law he sees his personal enemies. He nurtures his wrath, and wild thoughts of revenge fill his mind. His hate toward the persons directly responsible, in his estimation, for his misfortune—the arresting officer, the jailer, the prosecuting attorney, judge and jury—gradually widens in scope, and the poor unfortunate becomes an enemy of society as a whole. Thus, while our penal institutions are supposed to protect society from the prisoner so long as he remains one, they cultivate in him the germs of social hatred and enmity.

Deprived of his liberty, his rights, and the enjoyment of life; all his natural impulses, good and bad alike, suppressed; subjected to indignities and disciplined by harsh and often most inhumane methods, generally maltreated and abused by official brutes whom he despises and hates, the prisoner comes to curse the fact of his birth, the woman that bore him, and all those responsible, in his eyes, for his misery. He is brutalized by the treatment he receives, and by the revolting sights he is forced to witness in prison. What manhood he may have possessed is soon eradicated by the "discipline." His impotent rage and bitterness are turned into hatred toward everything and everybody, the feeling growing in intensity as the years of misery come and go. He broods over his troubles, and the desire to revenge himself grows on him. Soon it becomes a fixed determination. Society had made him an outcast: it is his natural enemy. Nobody had shown him either kindness or mercy; he will be merciless to the world.

Then he is released. His former friends spurn him; he is no more recognized by his acquaintances. Society points its finger at the ex-convict. He is looked upon with scorn, derision, and disgust. He is distrusted and abused. He has no money, and there is little charity for the "moral leper." He finds himself a social Ishmael, with everybody's hand turned against him—and he turns his hand against everybody else.

The penal and the alleged "protective" functions of prisons thus defeat their own ends. Their work is not merely unprofitable; it is worse than useless. It is positively and absolutely detrimental to the best interests of society.

There exists no other institution among the diversified "achievements" of modern society which, while assuming a most important role in the destinies of mankind, has proven a more reprehensible failure. Millions of dollars are annually expended for the maintenance of prisons—a great deal more than is spent on educational institutions in this country. That money could be invested with as much profit and less harm in government bonds of the planet Mars, or sunk in the Atlantic. No amount of punishment can obviate or "cure" crime so long as prevailing conditions, in and out of prison, drive men to it.

ANDER BERKMAN

SHOULD THOUGHT BE SUPPRESSED?

or do you approve of the sentiments expressed by **ALEXANDER BERKMAN** in his statement, in re deportation, made to the officials of the U. S. Immigration Service:

> I deny the right of any one—individually or collectively—to set up an inquisition of thought. Thought is, or should be, free. My social views and political opinions are my personal concern. I owe no one responsibility for them. Responsibility begins only with the effects of thought expressed in action. Not before. Free thought, necessarily involving freedom of speech and press, I may tersely define thus: no opinion a law—no opinion a

crime. For the government to attempt to control thought, to prescribe certain opinions or proscribe others, is the height of despotism.

Do you realize the menace of the Anti-Anarchist Law, under cover of which scores of men and women—not only Anarchists, but Socialists, I. W. W.'s, and ordinary workers—are arrested daily and held for deportation?

As **EMMA GOLDMAN** pointed out at her deportation hearing:

Under the mask of the same Anti-Anarchist law every criticism of a corrupt administration, every attack on Governmental abuse, every manifestation of sympathy with the struggling of another country in the pangs of a new birth—in short, every free expression of untrammeled thought may be suppressed utterly, without even the semblance of an unprejudiced hearing or a fair trial.

HELP US FIGHT THIS MENACE

EMMA GOLDMAN

Committee

ALEXANDER BERKMAN

Send Contributions to:

STELLA COMYN

36 Grove Street

New York

LEAGUE for the AMNESTY of POLITICAL PRISONERS

solicits your interest and financial support for its important work of securing an Amnesty for all political and industrial prisoners.

This **AMNESTY LEAGUE** also looks after the interests of political and industrial prisoners in various institutions, and supplies them with finances and with what little personal comforts prison rules permit. We ask you to contribute generously to our Prisoners' Relief Fund.

The **LEAGUE** also asks your co-operation to enable it to take care of the immediate needs of the women and children left without support because of the many and sudden arrests of radicals subject to deportation. Their need is very urgent.

LEAGUE FOR THE AMNESTY OF POLITICAL PRISONERS

Make checks payable to:

M. E. FITZGERALD

857 Broadway

New York

Send for Literature on Amnesty